FIRST SCIENCE LIBRARY
Super Materials

- 13 EASY-TO-FOLLOW EXPERIMENTS FOR LEARNING FUN
- ALL ABOUT THE AMAZING SUBSTANCES IN THE WORLD!

WENDY MADGWICK

ARMADILLO

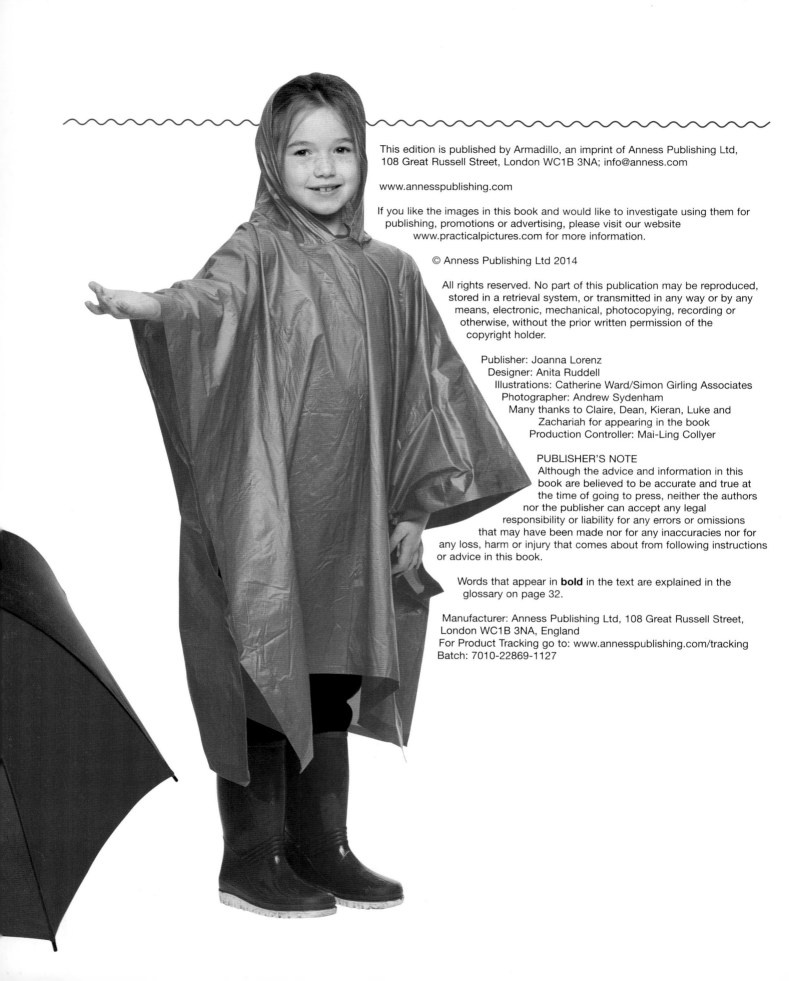

This edition is published by Armadillo, an imprint of Anness Publishing Ltd, 108 Great Russell Street, London WC1B 3NA; info@anness.com

www.annesspublishing.com

If you like the images in this book and would like to investigate using them for publishing, promotions or advertising, please visit our website www.practicalpictures.com for more information.

Publisher: Joanna Lorenz
Designer: Anita Ruddell
Illustrations: Catherine Ward/Simon Girling Associates
Photographer: Andrew Sydenham
Many thanks to Claire, Dean, Kieran, Luke and Zachariah for appearing in the book
Production Controller: Mai-Ling Collyer

Words that appear in **bold** in the text are explained in the glossary on page 32.

Manufacturer: Anness Publishing Ltd, 108 Great Russell Street, London WC1B 3NA, England
For Product Tracking go to: www.annesspublishing.com/tracking
Batch: 7010-22869-1127

Contents

Looking at materials

Materials such as metal, plastic, fabrics, wood, paper and glass are all around you. This book has lots of fun activities to help you find out about materials. Here are some simple rules you should follow before doing an activity.

- Tell a grown-up what you are doing. Ask him or her if you can do the activity.
- Always read through the activity before you start.
- Collect all the materials you will need.
- Make sure you have enough space to set up your activity.
- Follow each step carefully. Ask a grown-up to help if you need to.
- Watch what happens carefully and keep a notebook. Draw pictures or write down what you did and what happened.
- Never put any of the things you test in your mouth (except the chocolate rabbits you can make on page 27!)
- Always clear up when you have finished. Wash your hands.

► When rock becomes very hot, it **melts**. You can see streams of hot liquid rock pouring out of this erupting volcano.

What's what?

We use lots of different materials to make things. Some materials are made from plants or animals. Others are made from non-living things that are found in the ground.

▶ We use materials like bricks, wood and glass to build houses. You can make a tent from wood and plastic.

Sort them out

Collect the different things you can see in the picture. Put all the things made from plants and animals into one group. Put those made from non-living materials in another group.

brick

kitche foil

potte mug

glass

cotton blouse

silk scarf

spoon

leather shoe

paper

stones

wood

knitted glove

plastic bag

6

Toy tent

You will need: six small wooden canes, string, non-hardening clay, tray, sticky tape, pieces of plastic, round-ended scissors.

1 Get six small wood canes. Tie the tops together tightly with string. Put pieces of clay on the other ends of the canes.

2 Open out the sticks to make a cone shape. Press the clay on to a tray to keep the sticks steady.

3 Tape together pieces of plastic to make a big square. It should be large enough to cover the canes.

4 Cut a small hole in the middle of the plastic. Put it over the top of the sticks. Tape the plastic in place. Cut a flap for the door.

Touch and test

Materials are made from different things. They look and feel different. Some are better for certain jobs than other materials. We can make up tests to find out more about them.

Feel it

You will need: stone, smooth seashell, marble, bouncy ball, scouring pad, bath sponge, kitchen foil, furry scarf, silk scarf, paper, pencil.

Collect your objects. Gently rub their surfaces to feel if they are rough or smooth. Squeeze them to find out if they are soft or hard. Are they shiny or dull? Make a chart or draw pictures to show what you find.

	hard	soft	smooth	rough	shiny	dull
sponge		√		√		√

Carrying the can

We make carrier bags from paper, plastic and cotton. Let's find out which material makes the best bag.

You will need: string, paper bag, plastic bag and cotton bag (all the same size), two chairs, several food cans of the same size, round-ended scissors.

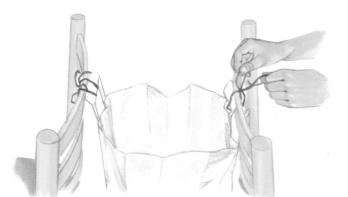

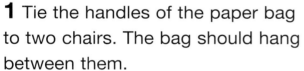

2 Put a food can into the bag. Keep adding cans until the bag breaks.

1 Tie the handles of the paper bag to two chairs. The bag should hang between them.

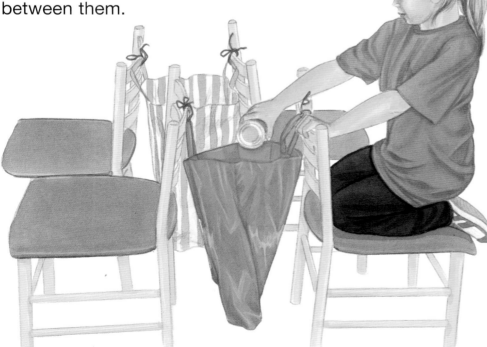

3 Now do the same with the plastic and cotton bags. Can the plastic bag carry more or fewer cans? Which bag can carry the most?

The cotton bag should be strongest and carry the most cans. The plastic bag should be stronger than the paper bag.

Stretch it

Some materials stretch when you pull them. When you let them go they spring back to their normal size and shape. You can have fun with these springy things.

Bend and stretch

You will need: rubber bands, straw, plastic ruler, non-hardening clay, copper wire, metal slinky, wooden spoon, plastic brick, hair band, balloon, paper, pencil.

Collect your objects. Pull them in turn to see which stretch. Do they spring back into shape? Gently bend them to see which bend.
Be careful not to snap them.
Make a chart of your results.

Spinning reel

You will need: two thin wooden sticks, rubber band, empty cotton reel, sticky tape, tray, non-hardening clay, plastic washer or a slice of candle, thin cardboard, pencils in various shades, round-ended scissors.

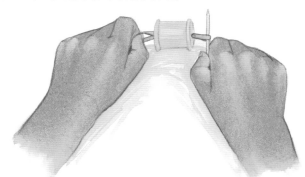

1 Put a thin stick through a rubber band. Push the other end of the band through the hole in a cotton reel.

2 Tape the stick in place on the outside of the reel.

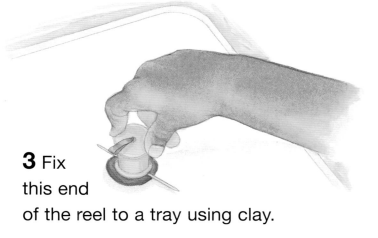

3 Fix this end of the reel to a tray using clay.

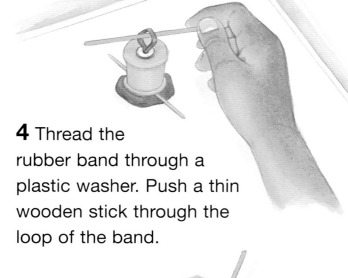

4 Thread the rubber band through a plastic washer. Push a thin wooden stick through the loop of the band.

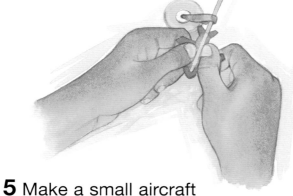

5 Make a small aircraft out of cardboard. Tape the aircraft to the end of the stick.

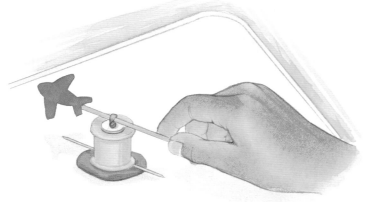

6 Turn the stick several times to wind up the toy. Let the stick go. Watch the aircraft spin around.

Metal mania

Metals are **mined** or dug out of the ground. Most metals are very strong. Some can be **moulded** into different shapes.

Look around your home and school. How many metal things can you find? Try to find out what metals they are made from.

▶ Copper can be pressed into shapes. It is also good for **conducting** heat and electricity. We can use it to make pots and pans, coins and water pipes.

▲ Steel is very strong. Knights wore suits made from plates of steel to protect their bodies in battle.

▲ Aluminium is light and strong. It is used to make drinks cans, kitchen foil and some aircraft.

Unbreakable mirror

You will need: cardboard, kitchen foil, thick clear plastic, sticky tape, ruler, round-ended scissors.

1 Cut pieces of cardboard, kitchen foil and clear plastic, all 10cm/4in by 8cm/3in.

2 Put the foil on the cardboard, shiny side up. Put the plastic on top.

3 Carefully tape around the edges to keep them all together.

Practical plastics

Plastics are not found in nature. They are made from **oil**. They are strong materials and can be moulded into many shapes.

We use plastics to make clothes, bags and toys. How many plastic things can you count here? Can you think of some other plastic things?

Wet or not?

What material would you use for a rainhat?

You will need: plastic, cotton, fine wool cloth, terry cloth, jam jar, rubber band, measure (a medicine cup is ideal), round-ended scissors, paper, pencil.

1 Cut out circles of plastic, cotton, wool cloth, and terry cloth. Make sure they are all the same size.

2 Stretch the plastic over the mouth of a jar. Pull it tight. Keep it in place with a rubber band.

3 Slowly pour 10ml/2 tsp of water on to the middle of the material.

What happens to the water? Does the water stay on the top, drip through or soak into the material?

Repeat with the other materials.

4 Make a chart to show what happens to the water.

	stay on top	drip through	soak in
cotton			
plastic			
wool cloth			
terry cloth			

The plastic does not let any water through. Of all the materials, it would make the best rainhat.

Wonderful wood

Wood comes from trees. We use wood to make furniture and in buildings. Paper is also made from wood.

Look at this picture. How many wooden things can you see here? Can you see some things made from paper? Paper is made from **wood pulp**. Look around your home. How many things are made from wood?

▲ We cut down trees and saw them into planks. The planks of wood are used to build things.

Mopping up

You will need: writing paper, kitchen paper, newspaper, brown paper, greaseproof paper, medicine cup as a measure, large bowl, round-ended scissors.

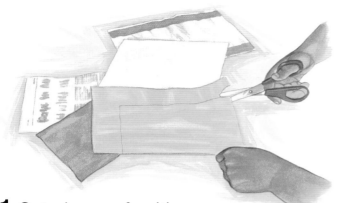

1 Cut pieces of writing paper, kitchen paper, newspaper, brown paper and greaseproof paper. Make sure they are all the same size.

3 Pour 10ml/2 tsp of water into a bowl. Mop up the water with the writing paper. Can it mop up all the water?

4 Dry the bowl and repeat with each kind of paper. Which paper is best at mopping up the water? Which paper is worst? Were you right?

2 Feel them. Which do you think will be best and worst at mopping up water?

The kitchen paper should be best. The greaseproof paper should be the worst.

Bouncing balls

Some materials bounce when they are dropped. Other objects do not – they are not bouncy.

▶ We use bouncy balls to play games.

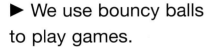

Collect a variety of balls and other objects, such as a rubber ball, a tennis ball, a wooden ball, a marble, a metal ball, an eraser, a golf ball, a plastic brick and a cardboard box. Squeeze them and feel what happens to them. Which objects do you think will bounce? Drop each object from the same height.

Which ones bounce? Were you right?

Bounce high

Which kind of ball will bounce the highest?

You will need: cardboard ruler, pencil, sponge ball, tennis ball, wooden ball, rubber ball.

2 Let a sponge ball roll off the edge of the table. Mark on the ruler how high the ball bounces. Repeat this with each ball.

1 Make a long ruler out of cardboard and mark it with centimetres or inches. Tape it to a table leg.

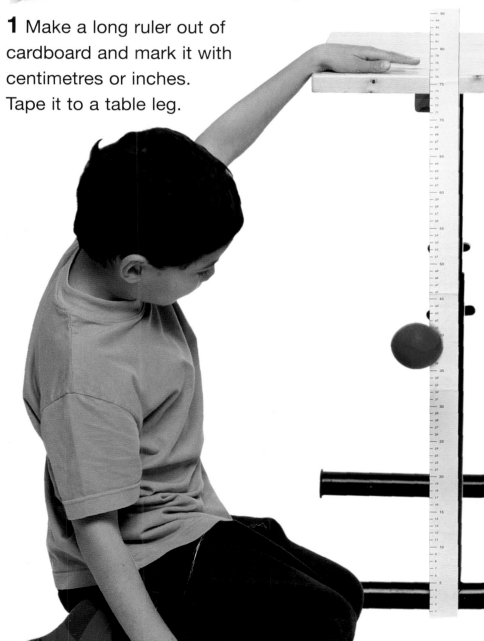

Which balls bounce the highest? How many times do they bounce? Are the second bounces as high as the first?

The sponge ball, tennis ball and rubber ball bounce the best. They bounce more than once. The second bounce is not as big as the first.

Float or sink?

Some materials **float** in water. Other more **dense** materials **sink**. We can make some materials float or sink by changing their shape.

You will need: bowl, water, stone or metal weight, wooden ball, coin, plastic brick, metal spoon, ball of non-hardening clay, foil food tray, paper, pencil.

Find a floater

Collect several objects as in the picture. Put the things in a bowl of water one at a time. Make lists to show which things float and which sink.

Shape changer

1 Put a ball of clay into a bowl of water. What happens? It sinks.

2 Take out the clay and dry it. Flatten it out into a thin sheet. Make it into a boat shape. Put it into the bowl of water. What happens? The clay boat floats.

3 Put a foil food tray in the bowl of water. What happens? The tray floats.

4 Carefully screw up the foil tray into a tight ball. Put it into the water. What happens? The foil sinks.

▶ This ship is made from steel. If it were made into a solid ball it would sink. It floats because the metal is spread out over a wide surface.

Kitchen chemistry

Everything in the world is made of **chemicals**. Even the food you eat is made of chemicals. Scientists who study chemicals are called chemists. You can be a kitchen chemist, and study the chemicals in the cupboard.

You will need: an adult helper, fresh red cabbage, sieve, knife and chopping board, pan of boiling water, jars, notebook, pencil, red and blue felt-tipped pens, dropper, range of test liquids and juices such as lemon juice, bicarbonate of soda (baking soda), milk, vinegar, fizzy cola, coffee and tea, strips of blotting paper (optional).

1 Ask a grown-up to chop the cabbage, boil it for about 15 minutes, and strain the water through a sieve. This will be your chemical indicator.

2 While the chemical indicator is cooling, put a little tap water into each jar. Get your notebook, pencil and pens ready.

3 Add about 15 drops of chemical indicator to each jar, using the dropper. Is it red or blue? Note this using the appropriate pen.

> Young children must be supervised in the kitchen, as some foods and liquids can cause sickness in large quantities. Chopping and boiling the cabbage should always be done by a grown-up.

4 Add one test liquid to a jar, such as a spoonful of juice squeezed from a lemon. Stir it in, and watch. Is it still red, or is it more like blue now? Note any change in your book.

5 Add another test liquid, such as a spoonful of milk, to the next jar. As before, mix it, and record any change in your book.

6 Add the next test liquid, such as a few drops of vinegar, to the next jar. Note any change. Do this with the other test liquids.

Acids, like vinegar or lemon juice, turn the cabbage water red or orange. Bases, such as baking soda, make it purple or blue. During the experiment, keep one jar that contains just the chemical indicator. Scientists call this a "control". You can compare the changes in the other jars with the appearance of the original in the "control" jar.

You could put a strip of blotting paper into each of your test jars. Write the name of the test juice or liquid on the paper. Then let the strips dry out and add them to your notebook.

Water works

Some materials change when added to water. Some seem to disappear. We say these materials **dissolve** in water. Others remain the same.

Clear or cloudy?

You will need: plastic cups, sugar, sand, flour, small plastic brick, kitchen foil.

1 Put a spoonful of sugar in a dry cup. What does the sugar look and feel like? It is shiny, dry and hard.

2 Pour 10ml/2 tsp of water into another cup. Add a spoonful of sugar and stir well. What happens to the sugar? The sugar softens, then disappears. It dissolves.

Repeat the steps with sand, flour, a plastic brick and some kitchen foil. Do they dissolve? No, they do not dissolve.

▲ This is sea salt. Sea water contains dissolved salt. The water **evaporates** in the hot sun. **Crystals** of salt are left behind.

24

Magic crystals

You will need: hot water, jug (pitcher), dessert spoon, washing soda, tall glass, thick cotton, pencil.

Children should not be left alone to do this activity. Great care is needed when using washing soda.

1 Ask a grown-up to pour 100ml/scant ½ cup of very hot water into a jug. Stir in a spoonful of washing soda. It will dissolve.

3 Tie a piece of cotton around a pencil.

2 Keep adding soda and stirring until a little soda remains undissolved at the bottom. Pour the liquid into a tall glass.

4 Balance the pencil across the top of the glass with the cotton in the soda **solution**. Leave the glass in a cool place for a few hours. What happens? Crystals of soda form on the cotton.

25

Solid or liquid

Some materials change when heated or cooled. Many metals and plastics melt when heated. They become **solid** again when they cool.

► This volcano is erupting. The rock inside a volcano is so hot that it melts. It bubbles out and flows down the sides of the volcano. The liquid rock cools in the air to form solid rock again.

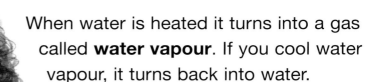

When water is heated it turns into a gas called **water vapour**. If you cool water vapour, it turns back into water.

When water **freezes** it forms a solid called ice. What happens when you heat ice? It turns back into water.

► **You will need:** cooking chocolate drops, butter, small bowl, large bowl, hot water, small rabbit-shaped mould, wooden spoon. You will need to cool things in the refrigerator.

Chocolate rabbit

We can use melted chocolate to make fun shapes.

1 Put some chocolate drops in a small bowl. Add a small knob (pat) of butter.

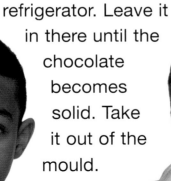

2 Ask an adult to pour some hot water into a larger bowl. Stand the small bowl in the bowl of hot water.

3 Stir the chocolate and butter until they melt.

4 Spoon the melted chocolate into a rabbit-shaped mould. Put it in the refrigerator. Leave it in there until the chocolate becomes solid. Take it out of the mould.

One-way change

Heat can make some materials change for good. They cannot go back to how they were.

▶ When wood burns, it turns into charcoal and ashes. Heat is given off. It cannot change back into wood.

Invisible picture

You will need: lemon juice, cocktail stick or toothpick, paper, a warm radiator to heat the paper.

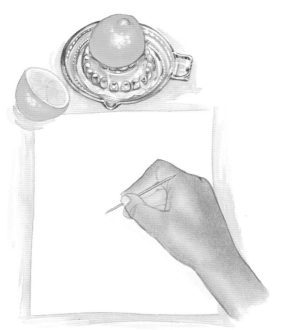

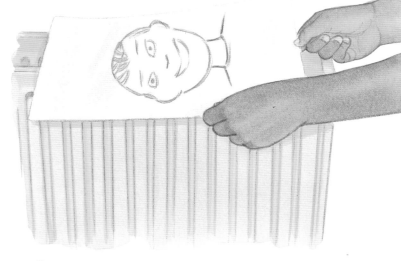

1 Dip a cocktail stick or toothpick into some lemon juice. Draw a picture on a piece of paper. Leave the paper to dry. The picture will be very hard to see.

2 Give the paper to a friend. Tell her to put it on a hot radiator. Your drawing will slowly turn brown so she can see it.

The picture appears because the dried lemon juice darkens when it is heated.

Fizzy mix

You will need: baking powder, tall drinking glass, vinegar, jug (pitcher).

1 Put a teaspoonful of baking powder into a tall glass.

2 Slowly pour on 100ml/ scant ½ cup of vinegar. What happens?

The mixture fizzes up to the top of the glass.
Baking powder is a **chemical**. The vinegar acts with the baking powder to make a **gas** called carbon dioxide. The fizzy froth is the gas bubbling up in the mixture. You cannot get the baking powder back again.

Hints to helpers

Pages 6 and 7

Discuss the different kinds of materials in the picture. Encourage the children to realize that the wool glove, cotton blouse, leather shoe, paper, silk scarf and wood are made from animals and plants. The plastic bag, metal teaspoon, brick, pottery mug, drinking glass, kitchen foil and stones are made from non-living materials.

Pages 8 and 9

Encourage the child to think of different ways to group the objects. Suggest other ways to test the strength of the materials, e.g. stretching, tearing and bending.

Pages 10 and 11

Explain that when things stretch they change shape. Introduce the word elastic and let children pull elastic or rubber bands to see how far they stretch. Make sure they don't let go of the bands near their faces. Find out how far a band can be stretched before it breaks or won't return to its original size. Talk about the uses of elastic things, such as trampolines, tyres and springs.

Explain that the wound-up rubber band has been stretched and has stored energy. As the band unwinds it turns the stick.

Pages 12 and 13

Ask the child to look at and feel different metals. Discuss what metals feel and look like – hard, cool, shiny, dull, smooth – are they all the same? Talk about what metals are used for – pans, radiators, coins, cutlery and ornamentation.

See if all metals behave in the same way if you try to pull, bend or stretch them.

Explain that most mirrors have metal in them. A thin layer of silver or aluminium under the glass makes a shiny layer.

Pages 14 and 15

Discuss what different plastics look and feel like – soft, hard, squashy, shiny, dull – and how they behave when they are pulled, squashed, stretched and bent. Discuss the many uses of plastics – to make spoons, clear film, furniture, etc.

Explain to the children that they have to keep everything the same and only change the material to make a fair test. Ask them to feel the materials and talk about when they would wear clothes made from each material. Ask them which material would be best and which one worst at stopping water going through. Explain why some materials let the water through. The cotton is not closely woven so lets the water pour through. The terry cloth soaks up the water and lets it drip through. Make sure the wool is pure wool and not acrylic. Water only drips slowly through the wool cloth because it is oily and so naturally waterproof. Mention that this helps sheep in wet weather.

Pages 16 and 17

Discuss the uses of different woods, e.g. to make furniture, pencils, doors and ornaments. Discuss how long trees take to grow and why we need to protect trees and forests.

Explain to the children that they have to keep everything the same and just change the material to make a fair test. Ask them to feel the materials and talk about which one will be best at mopping up water and why. Discuss why the kitchen paper was best: because the others are shiny, stiff or oily. Discuss why we need different kinds of paper.

Pages 18 and 19

Ask the children to handle and describe the texture of the balls. Encourage them to realize that the squashiness of a ball can affect the bounce. The hard rubber ball bounces best even though it is not very squashy. The sponge ball is very squashy but does not bounce as well. Solid non-squashy balls like the wooden ball do not bounce. A bouncy ball bounces again because as it hits the ground it is squashed and pushed upwards. As it springs back into shape, it is pushed up into the air.

Pages 20 and 21

Let the children push their flat hand slowly down into the water and feel the upthrust of the water pushing back. Encourage them to feel the objects before they put them in the water. See if they can guess which objects will sink. Objects that are heavy for their size will sink because the upthrust of the water cannot support them. Those that are light for their size will float.

The clay ball and screwed-up foil sink because the upthrust of

the water cannot support them. The foil tray and flat clay boat have a large surface area and the upthrust can hold them up.

Pages 22 and 23

Explain that acidic and basic (or alkali) chemicals are opposites. Chemists often need to know whether chemicals are acids or bases. If they do not know what the chemicals are, they should not taste them to find out, because many chemicals are poisonous. So chemists make special substances called chemical indicators, to test them.

Pages 24 and 25

Discuss substances that we use every day that dissolve or do not dissolve. Explain that substances that do not dissolve do not change in water. Talk about whether you can get the sugar back and link this with the picture of the sea salt. In the experiment, the sugar is the only material that dissolves. The flour is suspended in the water and makes a milky mixture with a layer of flour at the bottom. The flour will slowly settle at the bottom. The sand, plastic, wood and foil stay the same in water.

The soda dissolves in the water: you will need about four or five dessertspoonfuls in order to saturate the solution. When the solution cools, the water cannot hold so much soda. The soda turns back into a solid and a soda crystal forms on the cotton.

Pages 26 and 27

Discuss with the children how things change when heated. Talk about how water changes its state if it is heated or cooled. Discuss how we use melted metals to make things. Encourage them to understand that the materials change from solid to liquid, but they can change back again to their original form.

Pages 28 and 29

Encourage the children to understand that some materials cannot change back to their original form once they have been heated. Discuss how we use this in cooking, for example look at a raw and boiled egg.

Discuss how many items that we use have been made from something else and that we cannot get the original item back. For example, flour and eggs are made into cakes, potatoes into chips, wood into paper and chemicals into medicines.

Glossary

Chemical Any substance that can change when added to or mixed with another substance.

Conducting Letting electricity or heat pass through. Electricity or heat can pass easily through good conductors such as copper.

Crystals Solids with a certain shape. Salt crystals are shaped like cubes.

Dense An object is dense if it is heavy for its size.

Dissolve When some objects are added to a liquid they break down into tiny bits. They mix completely with the liquid so they cannot be seen.

Evaporates To change from a liquid or solid into a vapour or gas. When water is heated it changes into water vapour which rises into the air.

Float To stay on the surface of water or another liquid.

Freezes When a substance changes from liquid to solid in the cold. Water changes into ice when it freezes.

Gas A substance that has no fixed shape – unlike a solid. The tiny bits that make up a gas are spaced so far apart that they are not held together. They can move anywhere.

Melts To change from a solid to a liquid. When you warm ice, it melts into water. Some metals melt when you heat them.

Mined When materials are dug out of the ground.

Moulded Melted solids are moulded by pouring them into a special container. As the liquid hardens it takes on the shape of the container.

Oil A thick, black liquid found in the ground, formed from the remains of plants that died millions of years ago. Oil is used to make petrol and plastics.

Sink To go down into water or another liquid.

Solid A substance that has a definite shape that is not easy to change – unlike a liquid or gas. The tiny bits that make up a solid are tightly packed together. They are linked so strongly that they cannot move about.

Solution This is the substance made when a solid is dissolved in a liquid.

Water vapour Very tiny droplets of water in the air. They are too small for you to see.

Wood pulp Tiny bits of wood mixed with water to make a paste. This is used in the production of paper.